MY
ARCHAEOLOGICAL
MISSION TO
INDIA AND PAKISTAN

MY
ARCHAEOLOGICAL
MISSION TO
INDIA AND PAKISTAN

Mortimer Wheeler

THAMES AND HUDSON
LONDON

Filmset and printed in Great Britain by BAS Printers Limited, Wallop, Hampshire.

Contents

Preface

In August 1943 the Author was invited by the India Office and the
Viceroy of India (Lord Wavell) to undertake the total reorganization
of the Archaeological Survey of India, a task which was then regarded
as a matter of some unusual urgency. Whatever political and
technological pressures may have been at issue – and they turned out
to be of some considerable weight and complexity – were rendered
none the simpler by wartime involvements; and in fact it was not
until the Spring of 1944 that the writer was at last free to exchange
the vagaries of a brigade-command in the Eighth Army for the
fascinating amalgam of responsibilities which constituted and
continue to constitute the routine of the Indian Archaeological
Survey, ranging from the salvation of the Taj Mahal to that of the
sensitive vestiges of the Indus Valley Civilization. Years later it has
been considered that the somewhat elaborate processes and priorities
which comprised what is here memorized as *My Archaeological Mission
to India and Pakistan* may perhaps be thought worthy of a succinct and
essentially personal review.

1 Map of Indo-Pakistan subcontinent.

CHAPTER ONE

Introductory

This small book is a substantially personal account of the efforts made by many individuals since 1900 to organize and modernize the preservation and exploration of the ancient sites and monuments of the former Indian Empire prior to its dissolution and reconstruction after 1947. More briefly it may be described as a summary account of the latter phases of the old Archaeological Survey of India increasingly supplemented by the expanding enterprise of Indian and other universities under the spreading range of trained interest which has appeared internationally during more recent years.

Irrelevantly though it may seem, the account begins with a brigadier in a small military encampment on a hilltop above Algiers and the date is the beginning of August 1943. In the sunset the end of the day's planning operations of the forthcoming British and American invasion of Italy had drawn to its just close, when the Corps Commander, General Sir Brian Horrocks, dashed across towards my doorway with a signal in his hand and the remark, 'I say, have you seen this – they want you as – [reading] "Director General of Archaeology in India"! – Why, you must be rather a king-pin at this sort of thing! You know, I thought you were a regular soldier!' If the general ever paid an extravagant compliment, he did so then, although there was, I thought, a hint of pain and disillusionment in his voice. For my part the proposition was a complete bombshell. Without any sort of pre-warning, the India Office was asking for my release to take up a key post in a teeming country I had never been to in my life! However, I gathered my wits and said that I would consider the offer *after* the next battle but *not* before.

And so it eventually happened. In February 1944 I found myself imprisoned in a tiny cabin of the *City of Exeter* amidst the sprawling lines of a seven-knot convoy of about a hundred ships. Slowly we steamed westward from Britain as though seeking India in the track of Columbus, rounded the Azores, and veered east towards the African coast. The brilliant lights of neutral Tangier came up on the starboard bow as we groped darkly into the Mediterranean, and the trouble which it was easy to forebode broke upon us in daylight north of Algiers. For an hour successive waves of enemy torpedo-bombers came at us low over the water, and in the carefree way of maritime anti-aircraft gunners the air was filled dangerously with an infinitude of polychrome shells. Thereafter an eventless voyage took us to Bombay, and I stepped ashore with a mind full of ill-digested Indian history but with a pretty clear plan of campaign. Two days afterwards I took my seat comfortably enough in the Frontier Mail, bound for Delhi and Simla. The five-year mission had begun.

At this point it may be useful to recall both the short-term and the long-term circumstances which had thus combined to snatch me from the Italian war-front in 1943–4 to the more pacific frontiers of India on a cultural errand that is shown by contemporary record to have been regarded as one of some accumulative urgency. The main facts are as follows.

In March 1938 the Viceroy of India through the India Office had sought the advice of Sir Leonard Woolley on the constitution and operation of the Archaeological Survey of India which had notoriously at that time fallen into a considerable disrepute and was in no condition to cope with the aggrading needs and duties of an Empire steadily approaching the broadening responsibilities of home rule. In particular its astonishing wealth of architectural and archaeological monuments was such as to overstrain the financial and technological resources available or anywhere foreseeable at the time. True, as long previously as 1871 the Viceroy of the time had indeed appointed a Director General of Archaeology, after whose retirement in 1889 a successor was nominated, though in both instances responsibility was confined to research, record, and description, conservation being strangely excluded. A partial change occurred in February 1900 when, in consultation with the Secretary of State and the British Museum, the Viceroy, Viscount Curzon of Kedleston, whose interest in the art and archaeology of India was of an enduring penetration and quality which have ensured for him a lasting and outstanding place amongst the distinguished holders of his high office, proceeded to appoint a new Director General of the Survey with six archaeological surveyors for the prosecution of archaeological research, and, at last, for the conservation of listed remains. The Director General was to be J. G. Marshall of King's College Cambridge. Marshall subsequently worked closely and sympathetically with his Viceroy, but his lack of technical knowledge or interest led ultimately to the notorious breakdown of the Survey and to the resultant Woolley Report of February 1939, so that by 1943 even war

2 One of the main streets at Mohenjo-daro under excavation by J. G. Marshall in 1929–30.

3 R.E.M.W. in front of a captured German tank on the last day of the battle of El Alamein, 1942.

could not longer defer some sort of action and at the end of June the Secretary of State for India received a code telegram from the Viceroy (Lord Wavell) which included the following sentences: 'Post of Director General of Archaeology falls vacant next year and the Member for Education (India), after discussion with me, is extremely anxious to get a man from home for succession. I fear that condition of department is quite lamentable. It contains no one of any quality and level of its work is low. . . . I do not know if Mortimer Wheeler who I understand is as present serving in the Army would be possible.' The remainder of the story has been told.

CHAPTER TWO

Taxila and the North-west Frontier
1944

In the Introductory Chapter I left the new Director General of the
Archaeological Survey ensconced in the Frontier Mail en route for
Delhi and beyond on an initial journey of exploration and
introduction in the metropolis, the frontier zone and their environs.
His first major halt was at the town of Taxila, the ancient city of
Takshaśilā, some twenty miles from Rawalpindi, the modern
military base of the North-west Frontier. Thence the horizon was the
ultimate east-west barrier of the Himalayas with their massive burden
of winter snows brilliantly silhouetted against the grey Kashmir skies
or tumbling in a cascade of pastel colourings through the early-
morning mists of the marginal plain where the debris of the four
successive sites of the historic local capital of Taxila litters the fringe of
the basic lowland. Thereabouts in the first light of day the early
wanderer amongst the yellow mustard-crops casts his eyes upwards
to the remote skies where the solitary vulture peers distantly
earthwards in search of the morning meal. Thither too in the year 327
B C came the untiring Alexander from frontier conquests to which our
backward look will take us in due course; for it is there, in and about
the country of the river Indus and its tributaries, that our Indian
travelogue has its proper beginning.

At this time Alexander with the core of his travel-stained army had
been exploring the possibilities of enemy-resistance in the hills on his
north-eastern flank, whilst probing the way ahead towards the great
river and the populated kingdoms in the eastward plains beyond.
Amongst the primary obstructions to his advance, dominating the
broad encircling lowland now known as the Plain of Peshawar, once

4 (*overleaf*) Foothills of the Himalayas at dawn, as
seen across the site of ancient Taxila (Sirkap), 1944.

mostly as that of Gandhāra, stood the tall city-mound long accepted by modern scholarship as that of Pushkalāvatī or Peukelaōtis, alias 'City of Lotuses', then under the control of a lively and troublesome kinglet or governor named Astes, sufficiently formidable to demand special action from the invader. Accordingly, as we are told by the historian Arrian, a considerable task-force including half the Macedonian horse-guards and all the mercenary cavalry together with Indian auxiliaries was detailed to clear the way under the command of Alexander's experienced general Hephaistion. The fact that the ensuing siege occupied no less than thirty days is sufficient indication that the city was strongly defended and when in due course modern archaeology was brought to bear upon the problem, confirmatory evidence was not hard to discover.

Meanwhile, trial excavations had been carried out in 1902–3 without substantive result by J. G. Marshall at the beginning of his Director-Generalship. The towering mound or Bālā Ḥiṣār caught

5 View of the 'High Fort' or Bālā Ḥiṣār from the south-east, Chārsada 1958.

6 Portrait of J. G. Marshall, Lord Curzon's Director General of Archaeology in India who carried out the first trial excavations at Pushkalāvatī (Chārsada) in 1902–3.

Marshall's eye very naturally and vividly on his first visit to the Frontier, and its dominance may well have reminded him, fresh from his studentship in Greece, perhaps a little nostalgically of the Athenian Acropolis. He proceeded to dig a series of holes into the summit of the principal and adjacent mounds. But the task was too formidable a one for prentice hands, nor was the immense man-made mound of Pushkalāvatī at all comparable with the solid rock of the Acropolis. The enterprise was not renewed, but the newcomer in 1944 was led as a matter of priority to view the monumental earthwork which, looming over the provincial town of Chārsada, some eighteen miles north-east of Peshāwar, still commemorates the victorious progress of Alexander in 327 BC and incidentally the site of the first archaeological excavation, however inadequate, within the subcontinent, in 1902–3. The visitor found his way from Chārsada itself to the mighty mound completely blocked by about a hundred grunting buffaloes laden with double panniers filled with phosphatic earth obtained by the busy undercutting of the steep mound and so providing a fertilizing top-dressing for the vast sugar-plantation which spread like an inland ocean across the whole landscape. It took a meaningful watchman, armed with a rifle, in a country where the use of the weapon, even of the home-made variety, is fully understood, to halt and deviate the oncoming tide and so stop the headlong destruction of the mound. I was glad to find that over twenty years later the watchman or his successor was still at his post and that the wrecking of the phosphatic mound had completely ceased. But the 'High Fort' remained still a challenge to enquiry. When in 1944 I had drawn up for the Department an initial four-year programme for excavation in the subcontinent, Chārsada (alias Pushkalāvatī) had occupied the final place as a position of honour on my list and our work was due to begin there in the latter part of 1947. In August of that year momentous political events intervened. The then-new Pakistan Department of Archaeology, however, and the Pakistan Ministry of Education under which it operated had not forgotten the project and in 1958 invited me to take up the suspended task. The work was undertaken in November and December of that year as a preliminary reconnaissance with results which may here be conveniently interposed.

7 R.E.M.W. with his foreman, Sadar Din (left) and Dr F. A. Khan, one-time Director of Archaeology, Pakistan, on the first day of the excavation at Chārsada, 1958.

Our digging began with a stepped cutting some sixty feet deep down the face of the high mound in modern archaeological fashion to the basic level where a rivulet had been filled to the present surface by the injection of debris. Amongst this debris were the earthen bricks of a former internal barrier across which a one-time postern gate and rampart in timber and mud-brick had formerly been constructed doubtless when 'Astes lost his life and', as Arrian records, 'involved in his own ruin that of the town in which he had attempted to hold out'. Thereafter Alexander received the formal surrender of the city and installed a Macedonian garrison. Meanwhile we may imagine how the leader at the head of his motley army stood and surveyed the scene, his head set a little aslant on a sturdy neck and framed with stormy hair. In front of him a timber bridge built by his advance-party pointed to Further India whilst beside the bridge lay two thirty-oared galleys which had also been improvised for the crossing, amidst a scattering of native craft. But it was perhaps less at these things that Alexander was gazing than at the landscape on the opposite bank where, as far as eye could see, was stretched a seething mass of grunting oxen and bleating sheep, more than 10,000 of them, amongst which towered some 30 elephants, gay with paint and trappings. Nor was that all. In the foreground stood a small brightly apparelled group: Alexander sent to know their purpose; and word was brought back that an embassy awaited him from the king of Taxila, some forty miles away, 'the greatest of all cities between the Indus and the Hydaspes [or Jhelum]'. The king wished to submit the surrender of his metropolis and kingdom, and, as evidence of good faith, had added 200 talents of silver and this assortment of cattle. Then and there the Macedonian offered thanksgiving to his gods and a festival to his ever-hungry troops. Four years previously he had burned Persepolis, the Persian capital, and he now entered India as self-appointed heir to the Persian Empire. It was nearly two centuries since the Great King of Persia, Darius, had added this region to his dominions as his Indian Province, and the usurper was therefore claiming no more than his own by right of conquest.

8 (*above*) View west of the cutting down the side of the Bālā Ḥiṣār, Chārsada 1958.

9 (*opposite above*) View east from the top of the Bālā Ḥiṣār, looking down on the Chārsada cuttings, 1958. The defensive ditch built against Alexander was found in the final, easternmost, cutting.

10 (*opposite below*) Defensive ditch built against Alexander in 327 BC, with the post-holes for the postern (right) and bridge, Chārsada 1958.

Thereafter Alexander, led by his new host variously known as Āmbhi, Omphis or Taxiles, made his way south-eastwards, through the land which had been Persian territory as the twentieth and richest province of the Achaemenid Empire, towards what was now the Taxilan capital. Here, beyond a substantial tributary river, the Haro, and by two fertilizing streams of which one, the Tamrā or Tabrā Nālā was to enter the later classical literature of the West as the Tiberoboam or Tiberio-potamos, lay a small plateau 1200 yards in length nowadays known as the Bhīr Mound, on which the royal cicerone displayed to his guest the dun remains of his somewhat shabby metropolis partially revealed to modern eyes in its primordial crudity by many years of untutored excavation during the past half-century. To Alexander, with the trimness of his own Greek cities in mind, the relative indiscipline of the provincial village-capital no

11 (*left*) Portrait of Alexander. Greek, probably 2nd century BC, showing the conqueror about the time when he introduced history into India (*c.* 326 BC). Portrait head probably after Lysippus, in the British Museum.

12 Aerial view of Taxila I, the Bhīr Mound, 5th–2nd century BC. The irregular layout of the streets contrasts with the grid-plan of the Taxila School excavations in 1944 (right).

همه خورد نیستان پرمیوه دار   نخم میارستهٔ برکوبار   سکندرسیدازخواف خورد   ازآسایش ورور زیکایۀ نبرد   کزایران کیم خورشید زربود   ازخوردن وپشن زیربود   خرمند کفتای جهان کیر   کزرامکوبذنکایۀ نبرد   زهویمبرکیسی پذایۀ بر   زکرفر خوان نیست برکایۀ ہر   زپوشید هوزنکسترد نی   مهدبی نیازیم ازخوردنی

13 An 18th-century Indian miniature showing Alexander in discussion with the Brahmins or philosophers.

doubt presented an expressive contrast, alike in crafts, manners and customs, of which derivative classical raporteurs have preserved an intriguing picture amounting almost to an anthropological study.

In the market-place few save the most local wares were exposed. But in one quarter of it Alexander observed a throng of girls herded anxiously together and was told that they were of parents too poor to supply the necessary wedding-dowry and were therefore for sale in accordance with unquestioned custom. His host, turning perhaps to more serious matters, proceeded to tell him of certain philosophers who resided in a more honourable condition of poverty within the environs of the city. Alexander, prepared for all emergencies, summoned his own staff-philosopher, one Onesikritos, a Cynic, and bade him bring the Indian sages to the Presence. Onesikritos went off on his mission, and a circumstantial account of the ensuing episode has come down to us. His reception by the sages was, to say the least of it, a chilly one. One of them scornfully told him to remove his clothes and approach in proper humility. Another asked bluntly, 'Why has Alexander come all the way hither?' with the implication that he certainly had not been invited. Thus was Onesikritos summarily dismissed. The king of Taxila himself then intervened and eventually persuaded one of the sages to approach Alexander, to whom he proceeded to read a similar lesson. But the whole Taxila episode was clearly enlivened by a sustaining curiosity and interchange which can scarcely have been otherwise than the personal contributions of Alexander himself as he passed from scene to scene on his royally conducted visitation. In the market-place one of the Indian sages is recorded to have remarked, 'I commend the king [Alexander] because, although he governs so vast an empire he is still desirous of acquiring wisdom, for he is the only philosopher in arms that I ever saw'.

The prevalence of polygamy was noted, and the burning of widows (*sati*), as was the exposure of the dead to vultures in the Zoroastrian mode, and other habits of living and dying in a miscellaneous borderland society.

14 Aerial view of <u>Sh</u>aikhān, showing in 'ghost' outline the regimented plan of a 2nd-century BC Indo-Greek town.

CHAPTER THREE

The Taxila School of Archaeology
1944

But having accompanied the shadow of Alexander the Great into the beginnings of Indian history it is convenient to retrace one's steps for a moment along the stormy course of the conqueror's approach through the tumultuous country of the north-west frontier-zone and to arrive once more in the vicinity of Chārsada or Pushkalāvatī and more particularly at a tepé or city-mound known today as Shaikhān. At our request in 1958 the Pakistan Air Force had taken a remarkable air-photograph which showed in vivid outline about half a mile from the Bālā Hiṣār an appreciable part of a hitherto unknown grid-planned Indo-Greek city which survives today as a ghost-town,

15 The mound of Shaikhān in the middle distance, seen from the Bālā Hiṣār, Chārsada 1958.

consisting of straight main streets forty yards apart framing recognizable house-plans with a circular stupa set within a temple-precinct in the somewhat wider range of fifty yards, the whole plan consisting not of true walls but of robber-trenches from which the baked bricks of the actual walls had been removed by the villagers. Excavation has since confirmed that the plan was laid out by Indo-Greeks in the second century BC, following the urban traditions of the Greek world borne initially by the Alexander movement linking routes of conquest, exploration and commerce via Bactria and ultimately to India where the first rebuilding of Taxila (so-called Sirkap) was precisely of this kind. En route these and parallel vestiges of what may be called 'Asian Hellenism' have left their repeated mark: a Graeco-Roman seal-impression of the armed Athene from Pushkalāvatī; an alabaster Heracles from the same area; possibly a stone relief illustrating Laocoön and the Trojan horse; a bronze Harpocrates probably from Alexandria; a stucco satyr again in all likelihood from Egypt; fragments of Mediterranean glass and amphorae; and other classical oddments of which a number are preserved in the Taxila Museum.

16 Taxila II (Sirkap) from the air. The chessboard plan of this 1st-century-AD Parthian town (based on that of its Indo-Greek predecessor built two centuries earlier) may be contrasted with the haphazard layout of Taxila I (the Bhīr Mound), across the valley (Ill. 12).

17 A Graeco-Roman intaglio impression on clay of armed Athene; Chārsada, probably 1st century BC.

18 Bronze statuette of Harpocrates from Taxila II (Sirkap). The child-god raises his right forefinger to his lips in a gesture of silence. Probably originally from Alexandria, 1st century AD.

19 Stone relief from Gandhāra showing Laocoön and the Trojan horse, with Cassandra in Indian dress standing in the gate of Troy (left); 1st century AD.

20, 21 Stucco heads of a youth (*above*) and a bearded man (*left*) from Taxila II (Sirkap), 1st century AD, showing western Classical influence.

But now we must turn sharply onwards from 327 and 326 BC to the 1940s AD in the light of the exhortations of successive Viceroys, already cited, to stir the activities of the Indian Archaeological Survey from its unworthy condition of lethargy and archaism to a new and modernized phase of archaeological research and methodology. And here, at Taxila, amidst a useful assemblage of hutments and storehouses, including a well-conditioned local museum, accumulated over the years by the well-intentioned but too often desultory efforts of the under-trained Survey, opportunity and occasion stood awaiting adequate usage on the metropolitan site where, as we have already described, more than twenty-three centuries ago the rulers of west and east had forgathered in friendly and intelligent interchange. All that was now required by us in 1944 was the final urge for renewed co-operation in a modern context. That came in fact in the Spring of the year when, at an annual meeting (in Patna) of the nineteen vice-chancellors who then constituted the total hierarchy of the amalgamated universities of India, an urgent appeal was made for the recruitment of young university graduates for organized research into the neglected arts of India's archaeological technology.

The response was to me astonishing alike in quantity and quality and was almost instant. Within a few weeks more than sixty young graduates had assembled from all directions amidst the inviting facilities of Taxila and quickly settled down in an assortment of tents and huts prepared for their reception in accordance with traditional needs and usages. It might indeed be fair to claim that this was the last occasion in modern India when representatives of such a multiplicity of castes and other social variations voluntarily came together so earnestly on one spot with so unified an aim and fraught with so patent a sense of mutual good will. Such was 'The Taxila School of Archaeology, 1944', a tiny academic episode which those of us who shared in it like to remember with a certain pride and pleasure that may, in passing, be found worthy, perhaps, of the present casual but affectionate memorial. It was at least the first organized phase of a new Indo-Pakistan archaeology and the environment was a happy one.

22 The Taxila School of Archaeology, 1944.
Key to names, giving current or recent academic posts: 1 Dr P. Banerjee, Asst.
Director, National Museum, New Delhi; 2 Dr Ajit Mookerjee, formerly
Director, Crafts Museum, New Delhi; 3 Prof. S. R. Das, Dept. of Archaeology,
Viskwabharti University; 4 S. C. Chandra, d. 1961 while a superintendent of the
Survey; 5 Prof. B. N. Puri, Dept. of Ancient History, Lucknow University;
6 Prakhas Majumdar, formerly of the University of Calcutta; 7 B. K. Thapar,
Joint Director General, Arch. Survey of India; 8 Prof. A. H. Dani, Head, Dept.
of Social Sciences, Islamabad; 9 Dr D. R. Patil, formerly a superintendent of the
Survey; 10 Dr Bhanst, formerly of the Dept. of Sanskrit, University of Punjab.

23 Taxila School students drawing pottery, 1944.
Standing, second from left: Dr K. N. Puri, formerly Asst. Director, National Museum, New Delhi; seated, third from left: B. K. Thapar (see key to Ill. 22); centre, back to camera: S. C. Chandra (see key to Ill. 22); second from right: K. G. Goswami, formerly of thé University of Calcutta.

Briefly the Taxila School began in 1944 not unsuccessfully to deal on the one hand with the universal procedures of vertical stratigraphy and of grid-planning on the bases of detailed application, but on the other hand with the general principles of comparative chronology selectively illustrated from the fantastic abundance of material available in one way and another between the Mediterranean in the west and the world of China in the east, and incidentally both of them represented from local sources in the remote but fertile museum at Taxila itself.

But a more particular spur in this far-flung journeying was the collection in 1944 from a medley of literary and museological sources of the great number of recorded or otherwise accessible evidences of discoveries of Roman coins throughout the Indian subcontinent since 1775, not excluding a denarius of Tiberius actually from Taxila.

The general fact of the frequent occurrence of such readily identifiable intrusions into the Indian scene through several centuries, in a variety of contexts or even in none, had been vaguely accepted as a curiosity of historical movement but had never been analysed or adequately pursued for its comparative value as the possible basis of an exact chronology where a scientific association with otherwise undated Indian material might be established by experienced observation. This manifest problem was early presented to the new Taxila School, not as a primary experiment in northern India where such evidences were relatively rare, but as an inducement to turn east and southwards where, for example, more than fifty-seven such finds – single coins or hoards – had been noted from lands south of the Vindhyas alone. Indeed almost all first-century AD Roman coins or hoards from India not associated with later issues had been found in the Peninsula and the Dekkan, more precisely in Madras Province, Hyderabad, Mysore, Cochin, Pudukkottai and Travancore.

Accordingly, as a by-product of the Taxila School it was decided to make a systematic search on the basis of our coin-lists for sites where useful comparative Indian craftsmanship might reasonably be expected and brought to light.

In fact during the following months, two senior superintendents of the Archaeological Survey were sent systematically down the west coast from coin-site to coin-site to spy out the possibilities of further exploration. Immediate results were negative; but it so happened that one of us was fortuitously drawn at this time across to the east coast and found himself, not involuntarily, in Madras.

24 Four silver denarii of Augustus from a hoard found
at Eyyal, near Trichur, Cochin State, South India.

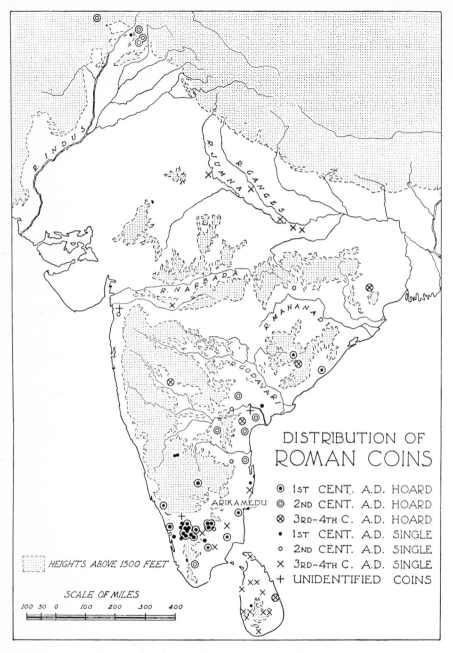

DISTRIBUTION OF
ROMAN COINS

⊙ 1ST CENT. A.D. HOARD
◎ 2ND CENT. A.D. HOARD
⊗ 3RD–4TH C. A.D. HOARD
• 1ST CENT. A.D. SINGLE
∘ 2ND CENT. A.D. SINGLE
✕ 3RD–4TH C. A.D. SINGLE
+ UNIDENTIFIED COINS

ARIKAMEDU

HEIGHTS ABOVE 1500 FEET

SCALE OF MILES
100 50 0   100   200   300   400

25 Map showing distribution of Roman coins in India.

His visit there coincided with that of a stray Japanese bombing plane which, weary of trailing its modest if potentially lethal load across the bay of Bengal, decided to discard it upon some obscure part of the ample target over which it now found that it had arrived. Resulting damage was not serious, but the incident was thought sufficiently alarming to encourage a widespread and sudden evacuation by a number of the more mobile residents. On arrival (on a hot May day) I discovered that these had included the staff of the Government Museum, which, as it happened, I had an untimely urge to visit. The absence of attendants was however by some ingenious measure circumvented and eventually I found myself a solitary wanderer in the empty halls of this provincial treasure-house, employing myself in the fashion wherein as an inveterate museum-man I am liable so to do; in other words seeking out the odd places and recondite cupboards where the less familiar secrets may be thought to find concealment. And in an instant my steaming forearm on a sweat-laden morning found its way into a deep recess where my hand closed with almost uncanny sensibility upon what – yes! – could only be the elongated neck and parallel handles of a Roman amphora, long devoid of the content with which it had one time been hospitably supplied.

Tireless questioning led to the conclusion that the amphora had been extricated from a site on the outskirts of Pondicherry, then the capital of French India, some eighty-five miles south of Madras, by local French antiquaries, and that excavations of unknown productivity were said to be still there in progress. Following a telephone conversation, the questioner travelled by the night-train to Pondicherry, to be met, in the absence abroad of the French Governor, by a large posse of the official staff and taken warmly in charge. The immediate rendezvous was the city's soi-disant hostelry where in the rapidly growing heat of the early tropical morning the miscellaneous assembly focused upon an equally miscellaneous breakfast with a determined background of somewhat unseasonable cognac enlarged by a vivacious general conversation.

26 Roman Arretine ware from Arikamedu, near Pondicherry, South India. The sherd bottom right is an imitation Arretine form.

In due course the guest of the occasion brought matters to a more professional point with an enquiry as to the possible existence of a city museum which he might perhaps have the honour of visiting under this distinguished escort? The reply was dubious. There was not a museum as such, but there was a library, with assorted glass cases which might fall within the range of my interests. Would I care to venture? . . . Now suitably or less suitably refreshed our very mixed little party trooped through the French-provincial streets and eventually reached an undemonstrative building full of stacked books and newspapers. And, fair enough, amidst the medley was a scatter of closely set cases with glass lids thickly covered in dust.

I went up to a covered case and swept a sweaty forearm across the glass. The result might be described as electric. Where there had just previously spread an impermeable layer of dust was now displayed a considerable crust of fragmentary Graeco-Roman amphorae, and amidst them were sherds of red ware of the sort that any student of things classical could readily recognize as pieces of the distinctive pottery that barely two millennia ago had issued profusely from the kilns of Tuscany or elsewhere in central Italy, notably from Arezzo whence under the common name 'Arretine', came the famous ware which today may still be uncovered in Roman London or early Verulamium on the other side of the world. And now here at last in Pondicherry was journey's end; precisely those ancient and dateable fabrics in a context which in southern India gave them and their associations a new meaning to us in time and space. They opened in fact a new field in the broad world of comparative archaeology.

There can indeed be no question that the successive identifications of Roman wares at Madras and Pondicherry in 1944 together constitute the most important discovery noted in the present book, if not in the total story of recent Indian archaeology. As such they merit further treatment in a separate chapter.

27 View north-east across the lagoon to the site of the Indo-Roman trading-station at Arikamedu, South India, 1945.

28 Indo-Roman foundations projecting from the river-bank at Arikamedu, 1945.

CHAPTER FOUR

Arikamedu

An Indo-Roman trading-station
on the east coast of India

Subsequently to the first dramatic moment of recognition in the Pondicherry library we were conducted to the study of a Brother Faucheux who, in collaboration with the Chief of Public Works, had for a few years previously carried out fairly deep but unmethodical excavations on or behind the foreshore of the former estuary (now a lagoon) of the Gingee river some two miles south of Pondicherry at and near a spot where brick walls with potsherds obtruded from the flanks or surface of the present water-side bank. Some years still earlier attention had been drawn to the area as one of potential occupation in the Roman period by another French antiquary, one Jouveau-Dubreuil, to whom the local children had been accustomed to bring salvaged gem-beads amongst which one was reported to have borne a head of Augustus in intaglio, inducing the enthusiastic recipient to exclaim, 'Nous avons là une véritable ville romaine'. Be that as it may, subsequently enough classical material had accumulated to show Roman or Romanized occupation hereabouts approximately from the end of the first century B C to the latter part of the first century A D.

It was time for action, and the French authorities were amiably complaisant. From April to June in 1945 the Archaeological Survey of India would take over the archaeology of the area, with the now considerable weight of the sixty Taxila students, by this time appreciably trained, behind it. The North marched South; and the

43

erratic cuttings of our French predecessors on the scene were methodically superseded and extended by school-trained grids and graduated stratigraphy in the busy hands of students already trained to anticipate just this sort of situation – the emergence of familiar western products in meaningful association with the still-unknown and variable output of the east. From village-usage our growing

29 Excavations in progress, Arikamedu 1945: Taxila School students applying the grid method.

Graeco-Roman site was shortly known to ourselves and our cheerful peasant-workpeople as Arikamedu;[1] alternatively the name Viram-patnam was borrowed from that of a small fishing-village which, with its string-tied boats, marked the line of breakers half-a-mile away. The foreground, under treatment, rapidly assumed something of the aspect of our disciplined Taxila, with precaution as the order of

[1] Possibly = Arrukkumēdu = 'Mound of ruins'; or Arukumēdū = 'Mound on a river bank'.

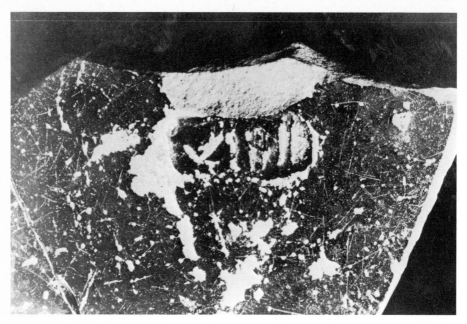

30 Detail of a sherd of Arretine ware, showing the Italian potter's stamp, VIBII or VIBIE. Found at Arikamedu, 1945.

the day. The over-all purpose, the archaeological reason for our Arikamedu, was that of serious confrontation between the known and the unknown. Progress must be patient and slow and completely certain. It might be at least a dozen or fifteen days before real progress could be registered. In fact the moment of triumph did not arrive until the twelfth day, and when it did arrive it was at once memorable and has become itself a key-date in the archaeology of Peninsular India.

A deep squared pit was being driven down to the tide-level through wet sand and estuarine silt when the supervisor, who happened to be one of our South Indian students, splashed suddenly from his pit with a large and muddy sherd in an upraised hand. I took the sherd from him, and a dip in the pool at the bottom of the pit was enough. The sherd was a large piece of the flat base of a dish of reddish ware with the mud-filled stamp of the maker in Roman lettering on

46

the inner side. To cut the story short, a rubbing of the stamp was sent post-haste to the most knowledgeable of my correspondents in Oxford, Miss M. V. Taylor, and in an astonishingly brief space of time the reply came back to me in my jungle-shaded bungalow a mile from where we were working. The subsequent report in *Ancient India*, number 2 (1946) is worth repeating: 'VIBII – (probably VIBIE, possibly VIBIF). On the interior of the flat base of a dish, form uncertain, found on Site AKII, layer 7Ar. There seem to have been two families of Arezzo potters, the VIBII and the VIBIENI, to the latter of whom the stamp would appear to belong.' Miss Taylor had spent much time in looking up the appropriate literature at Oxford, and the following is a summary of her discoveries.

The potteries of the Vibieni at Arezzo were near those of M. Perennius and P. Cornelius by S. Maria in Gradi, and worked both before and after them. On the death of C. Vibienus, his sons succeeded to the industry. What their relation was with the pottery of 'Vibius' is not clear, or which employed the other, but the Vibieni and Vibii descended from an ancient Etrurian family, the Vibia, whose name is still preserved in Bibbiena.[2]

It would seem therefore that members of the Vibia family were producing Arretine or related pottery from the beginning of the first century BC until after the middle of the first century AD.

Other Roman stamped sherds occasionally occurred at Arikamedu. My notes record that the small area excavated there in 1945 yielded 31 fragments of this *terra sigillata* or 'Arretine ware' whilst a score or more of additional pieces have been found before and since that year, but for the most part the ware is extremely scarce in India. On the other hand 116 sherds of classical amphorae emerged from the restricted area just referred to, although the presence of the type was almost universal on other Arikamedu sites, the inference being that the importation of the amphorae continued throughout the occupation of the town as otherwise excavated.

But alongside these and other imported variants have occurred a number of more local types which share their dates by virtue of association. In particular a recurrent type was first recognized in 1945

---

[2] See Gamurrini in *Notizie degli Scavi* (1883), pp. 451ff. For related evidence see also Loeschcke in *Mitteilungen der Altertums-Kommission für Westfalen*, V (1909), p. 186, showing that the Vibii flourished before the occupation of Haltern in 11 BC–AD 16.

31 Fragments of Roman amphorae from the Mediterranean found at Arikamedu, 1945.

32 Rouletted ware from Brahmagiri, Chitaldrug district, Mysore. This type of pottery, showing Mediterranean influence, is distributed widely across South India and was found associated with Arretine ware at Arikamedu.

at Arikamedu alongside Italian Arretine ware and elsewhere with Roman coins of the first centuries B C–A D and thereby became what geologists call a 'type fossil', of widespread utility as a time-index over central and southern India. Its characteristic shape is a dish, sometimes more than twelve inches in diameter with an incurved and beaked rim and two or three concentric rings of rouletted pattern on the flat interior base. The pattern is not an Indian feature and is certainly derived, like the associated Arretine, from the Mediterranean. The fabric is grey or black, and has often a remarkably smooth surface; it is usually thin, brittle and well burnt, with almost a metallic ring. The better examples are doubtless imported, cruder varieties seem to be local imitations. The ware, though widespread, is particularly characteristic of the South Indian areas reached by Roman trade in the first and second centuries A D. It is commonly known as 'rouletted ware'.

From its first recognition a deliberate search has been maintained for occurrences and associations of this key ware as a primary archaeological index of cultural progress throughout the Peninsula from Ceylon to the river Kistna and beyond, commonly, as indicated, in steady linkage with the distribution of Roman coinage in spite of the accidental absence of that articulate witness from the point of initial contact.

The distribution of the coins – mostly of Augustus and Tiberius – and the approximately contemporary rouletted ware, is noteworthy and has been widely indicated and discussed.[3] Incidentally it is noteworthy that, although a majority of Roman coins from India are derived from coastal sites, a few Roman hoards and single coins have been found 200 miles or more from the sea, e.g. in northern Mysore, in situations comparable with those recorded for the rouletted ware.

Lastly we must turn from village place-names, from alien borrowings and even from repetitive idiosyncracies to the straight question of the traditional relationships of Arikamedu or Pondicherry in their classical environment as an integral part of the map and economy of India in the Roman world. The problem does not in fact

---

[3] See *Ancient India*, number 2 (Delhi, 1946), pp. 45ff.

appear on broad consideration to present any insurmountable difficulty.

The *Periplus of the Erythraean Sea*, a remarkable handbook written by an anonymous Greek merchant in the first century AD, after referring to Kolkhis or Korkai, the ancient pearl-port near the southern end of India, mentions the three principal markets and anchorages to which resorted the merchants of 'Limurikē', probably the region otherwise known as 'Damirika' (the Peutinger Table) and 'Dimirica' (the Ravenna Geographer) and etymologically equivalent to the *Tamil*-land. The three ports (from the context, south to north) are *Camara, Podoukē, and Sōpatma*. Ptolemy (*Geography* VII, 1, s.14) refers to 'the mouth of the river Khabēros', clearly the Kāverī, and *Khabēris emporion* which may safely be identified with Kāverīpatnam or Kāverīppattinam, the modern Tranquebar, familiar in Tamil literature as a port frequented by foreign merchants, and mentions *Sabouras emporion* (unidentified) and *Pōdoukē emporion*. He is also working northwards, so that Pōdoukē must be somewhere to the north of Kāverīpatnam. Whether, as Müller suggested, Ptolemy's *Khabēris* should be equated with the *Camara* of the *Periplus* is less certain; but the *Sōpatma* of the *Periplus* has with some plausibility been identified with the Sō-pattinam of Tamil literature, the modern Markāṇam, on the coast between Pondicherry and Madras.[4]

All that can be inferred from this is that the geographical position of Arikamedu (Pondicherry) is consistent with the general indications given for Podoukē or Pōdoukē by the *Periplus* and Ptolemy. The site lies sixty miles north of Tranquebar and twenty miles south of Markāṇam. Moreover, Pondicherry is a European corruption of *Puduchchēre*,[5] meaning 'Newtown', and it can at least be claimed that the Greek Podoukē is as near to this as is the modern French Pondichéry.

There the nominal evidence at present ends. But the new identification of a Roman emporium in the immediate vicinity of Pondicherry gives a fresh and seemingly conclusive weight to its equation with Podoukē – an identification which has already been suggested by more than one writer.[6]

[4] K. A. Nilakanta Sastri, *The Cōḷas* (University of Madras, 1935), I, 30.
[5] *Hobson-Jobson* cites an English reference to the place in 1680 with the spelling 'Puddicherry'.
[6] See W. H. Schoff, *The Periplus of the Erythraean Sea* (London, etc., 1912), p.242.

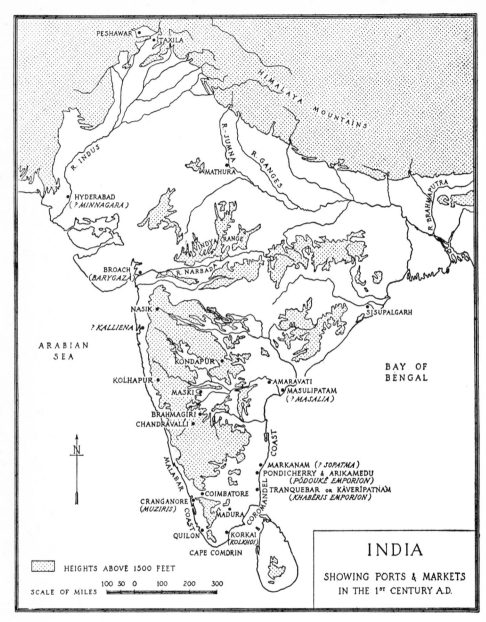

33 Map showing ports and markets in the 1st century AD.

Merchant navigation in the Roman world

Now that Chapter Four has included a preliminary mention of the *Periplus of the Erythraean Sea* within the historico-geography of the Indian Peninsula it is proper that Chapter Five should turn to some account of the astonishing achievements recorded by this daring and knowledgeable Greek merchant in varying circumstances on the high seas between Egypt and China. His famous book has been well described as a 'geographical landmark' of the first order and as 'one of the most fascinating books that have come down to us from antiquity'. At least with sporadic aid from Pliny and other geographers, the *Periplus* preserves a vivid general picture of the adventurous and elaborate navigation which enabled the Roman Empire to dominate an appreciable part of the world's commerce overseas for several centuries. Here a few selections from the factors involved must suffice an abbreviated context.

About the month of July, the Etesian winds, otherwise the south-western monsoon, bring the summer rains to India, where they last until September. By keeping them on the quarter, the sailors from the ports near the mouth of the Red Sea were able to steer straight across the approaches to the Persian Gulf quite away from the Indus delta and Broach. Similarly those making to South India who have sailed a little south of east across the Arabian Sea, have in favourable circumstances made the long voyage towards Muziris, as Pliny tells us, in forty days. 'Hippalus', adds the *Periplus*, with tantalizing brevity, 'was the pilot who, by observing the location of the ports and the condition of the sea, first discovered how to lay his course straight across the ocean'. So much, if too little else, the famous

Greek merchant-sailor tells us about one of the greatest names in the history of navigation. But when Hippalus actually flourished is still arguable, though if we accept the indication of Strabo that before AD 21 no fewer than 120 ships sailed for India from Myos Hormos on the Red Sea, it would appear that maritime organization had already achieved a formidable measure of advancement under the unification of Augustus (23 BC–AD 14) or at least by the time of the recorded reception of two or more Indian delegations by Augustus about 25–21 BC, either of which might provide a viable context, if not for the actual discovery of the 'Hippalus' or monsoon, at least for its diffusion beyond the corporations of Arab sailors and other agents who may be supposed to have monopolized the Indian traffic thitherto.

For the rest it will suffice here to note that an organized and circum-continental interchange involved a professional understanding of the periodicity and moods of the monsoons linked with and extended by cross-country and coastal trafficking between the Malabar anchor-ages on the one hand and the multiple estuarine Coromandel services with their oriental frontages on the other.

Suffice it that the classical geographers and the Tamil literature of the 'Śaṅgam' age have familiarized historians with the outlines and some of the details of Indian trade with the west in and after the first century AD. At its prime, the trade was extensive. It included as Indian exports, pepper, pearls, gem-stones, muslin, tortoise-shell, ivory and silk; and as imports from the west coral, lead, copper, tin, glass, vases, lamps, wine and, at first, a multitude of coined money.

Of these various commodities it is difficult not to single out with Pliny (*Natural History*, XII, 14) the Malabar pepper which filled the Pepper Barns beside the Tiber as a primary function of Roman trade with the Orient. Pliny is eloquent on the subject:

It is quite surprising that the use of pepper has come so much into fashion, seeing that, in other substances which we use, it is sometimes their sweetness and sometimes their appearance that has attracted our notice; whereas pepper has nothing in it that can plead as a recommendation in either fruit or berry, its only desirable quality being a certain pungency; and yet it is for this that we import it all the way from India! And who, I wonder, was the man that was not content to prepare himself by hunger only for the satisfaction of a greedy appetite.

With somewhat wider foresight Pliny might have anticipated that Alaric the Goth was to demand 3,000 lbs of pepper in his treaty with the Romans in AD 408. There for the moment we may pause . . . but only to turn back in our list to the infinitely knowledgeable Pliny, who reminds us (*Natural History*, VI, 101) that 'in no year does India absorb less than fifty million sesterces', an extraordinary efflux such as Tiberius may have had in mind when he complained to the Roman Senate of the reckless exportation of money.

But on the assumption that Tiberius's budget-figures were approximately correct the question inevitably rises in the mind of the listener: how was this seemingly extravagant export-cash utilized effectively *in partibus orientalibus*? Broadcast exchange was scarcely in question, for in no part of India was there any viable interrelationship of coin-values, any considerable native currency of gold or silver to which the Roman coinage could be approximated in market-practice. As late as the second century AD, in the time of Pausanias, it is recorded that the Indians exchanged their wares with those of the Greeks 'without understanding the use of money'. The potin or lead struck by the Āndhra Empire of central India in the first two centuries AD implies a certain understanding of the monetary principle and may so have been incidental to the occasional introduction of gold and silver Roman coins (aurei numerous but denarii predominating)[1] brought no doubt from Malabar on the west and by way of the Coromandel coast and the river-system on the east, although be it repeated and emphasized that a generally productive and accessible site such as our 'Arikamedu' on the Coromandel coast has so far failed to yield a single Roman coin to extensive and often meticulous excavation, and we there still fall back on specific ceramic evidence. For the rest the numismatic aspect of our evidential problem has an alternative answer which I find for the most part fully satisfactory. It is sufficiently evident that the imported coinage, consisting exclusively of gold and silver, was employed normally in the Indian

[1] W. F. Grimes (ed.), *Aspects of Archaeology, Essays presented to O.G.S. Crawford*, (London, 1951) pp. 345–81.

traffic not as currency but as bullion weighed in exchange for goods, like bullion in an Indian bazaar today.

Unhappily not one of the identified Indo-Roman trading stations or *emporia* has yet been sufficiently excavated to reveal its extent, shape or substance. Apart from assemblages of pottery and other small finds discovery has largely been confined to *disjecta* which rarely combine into any life-size and coherent picture. For that we are still primarily dependent upon the grace and curiosity of the Tamil poetry of the earlier centuries AD, without which much of our story would be an arid one indeed. Often but not excessively cited is the famous epic known as *The Lay of the Anklet (Śilappadikāram)*, which describes the quarter of the east-coast city of Puhār or Kāverīppaṭṭinam, almost certainly Ptolemy's *Khabēris emporion* at the mouth of the Kāverī river. 'The sun', proclaims the poet, 'shone over the open terraces, over the warehouses near the harbour and over the turrets with windows like the eyes of deer. In different places of Puhār the onlooker's attention was caught by the sight of the abodes of Yavanas, whose prosperity never waned. At the harbour were to be seen sailors from many lands, but to all appearances they lived as one community . . .' And Tamil rajas employed bodyguards of western mercenaries, 'the valiant-eyed Yavanas whose bodies are strong and of terrible aspect' and who, equipped with 'murderous swords', were 'excellent guardians of the gates of the fort-walls'. Yavana craftsmen were also sought after in southern India, especially for the manufacture of siege-engines. Indeed the term 'Yavana' and its parallel 'Yonaka' occur abundantly in our Indian literature, implying normally a westerner in the fullest meaning of the word and emphasizing the dominance of the European element, equivalent to 'Ionian', i.e. Greek, not merely in the South but as far north as the region of Bombay; for instance in a Prakrit inscription on a Buddhist cave approximately of the first century BC or AD at Nasik and in eight or more other inscriptions of the same area recording dedications of donors who may describe themselves as Yavanas but sometimes bear Indian names. In the present context it may be supposed that these Indian donors or their forebears had come from cities in the former Indo-Greek kingdom further north, and in the present circumstances may be thought to presume a certain preparedness on the part of wealthy Indian merchants of the first centuries BC–AD for further contact with the western world.

Semi-finally, as bearing more directly again upon two-way trade with the South, may be quoted from Tamil poems of the Śangam age: 'Agitating the white foam of the Periyaru, the beautifully built ships of the Yavanas came with gold and returned with pepper, and Muziris responded with the noise.' And in another poem a Pāndya (South Indian) prince is exhorted to drink 'the cool and fragrant wines brought by the Yavanas in their vessels'. The universal abundance of Mediterranean amphorae at Arikamedu (or Podoukē) may provide an unsought archaeological footnote to the poet.

Alternatively, turning back ultimately from poetry to archaeology, a parting reference may be made to the rambling brick building, now 150 feet long, which constitutes the Archaeological Survey's elaboration of two somewhat summary pits sunk in 1941 by our French antiquarian friends into the foreshore close to the eastern edge of the lagoon. The structure acceptably represents a massive warehouse such as those already picturesquely recalled at Puhār, no doubt of a kind characteristic in general of the east-coast emporia. The Arikamedu building appears to have been occupied in the first and second centuries AD and to have been extensively despoiled for bricks in the Middle Ages and later. Its immediate environs include two walled courtyards associated with carefully built tanks supplied and drained by brick culverts and thought, on modern South Indian analogies, to have been used in the preparation of the muslin cloth which has from ancient times been a notable product of this part of India.

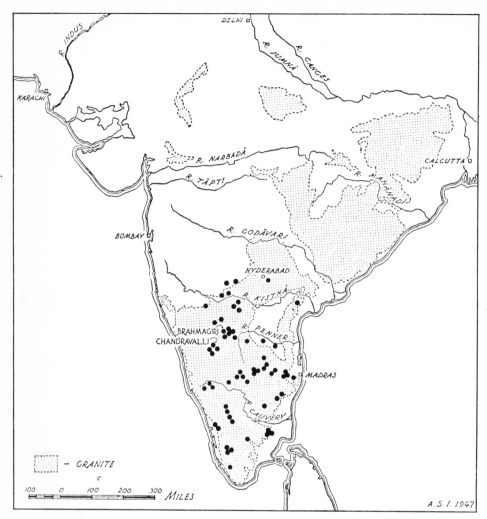

34 Map showing distribution of megalithic cists with 'port-holes'.

CHAPTER SIX

Indian megaliths

An elderly antiquary may be forgiven for turning inevitably backwards towards that classic of the Victorian age of studentship – James Fergusson, F.R.S., *Rude Stone Monuments* (London, 1872) – with the opening sentence of its chapter on 'India':

> The number of rude-stone monuments in India is probably as great as or even greater than that of those to be found in Europe, and they are so similar that, even if they should not turn out to be identical, they form a most important branch of this enquiry. Even irrespective, however, of these the study of the history of architecture in India is calculated to throw so much light on the problems connected with the study of megalithic monuments in the West that, for that cause alone, it deserves much more attention than it has hitherto received.

That paragraph holds the nucleus of more than one involved argument, but for present purpose it may be allowed to stand imperturbably very much as and where it stood in Fergusson's day.

No comprehensive survey of the Indian megaliths and their related monuments has yet been achieved, although in fact the Archaeological Survey in its new guise had turned to their manifest problems before its extending arm had reached southwards to Pondicherry and the emergent Indo-Roman picture with which we have been concerned in recent chapters. Again it was Madras and its environs that pointed the way as early as the year 1944. The district of Chingleput by Madras caught the interest of a specialized officer of the Survey with a Cambridge training who was encouraged to initiate a systematic survey of megaliths in the Madras region. That project is still incomplete, but useful preliminary instalments have been partially published in the periodical *Ancient India* and general

35 Megalithic granite cist with 'port-hole', Vengupattu, North Arcot district.

interest in the subject has been widely spread. The main bulk of the south Indian megaliths is ancient and lies to the south of latitude 18, which runs a little north of Hyderabad (Deccan) and is characteristic of peninsular India.

A recurrent type is a cist built of rough granite blocks, now above ground, within a circle of similar blocks which enclose an area 30–140 feet in diameter. The uprights, four or more in number, are (or were) covered by a massive single or double capstone covered in turn by a low cairn. The eastern upright is often pierced with a 'port-hole' $1\frac{1}{2}$–2 feet in diameter approached externally by a downward ramp flanked by orthostats or dry-stone walling. When the main deposit of funeral pottery and other objects (ironwork, beads, whorls) had been laid on the floor-slab the bundles of excarnated long-bones and skulls (up to six) were introduced apparently through the port-hole, which was also the ingress for subsequent offerings prior to ultimate sealing.

But in considering the generality of Indian megaliths it is well with Professor Fürer-Haimendorf to separate features which usefully distinguish the ancient megalithic monuments now under study from the partially comparable assemblages which have survived amidst living tribal cultures of unknown antiquity further north and east. A primary differential lies in the question of usage. For example the megaliths of the tribal folks of today are commonly memorials unconnected with graves or burning-grounds, whilst those of prehistoric times are in the main graves or closely associated with graves; appropriately the distinctive port-hole opening which we have described as characteristic of most of the ancient megalithic cists

36 A 'port-hole' megalithic cist with grave-goods still in place, excavated at Brahmagiri, 1947–8.

of southern India does not occur amongst any of the tribes of middle India who bury their dead in megalithic graves, such as the Mundas and Hos.

And if we add to these various diversities and difficulties the almost complete geographical exclusiveness of the two great groups (central and north-eastern), their essential separateness is at present a fair premise. In summary, despite occasional and only partial analogies, the differences between the megaliths of the tribal areas and the ancient tombs of the Deccan and peninsular India are far more impressive than their resemblances.

Amongst the various objectives on which we have touched it was in fact the presence of almost unnumbered megaliths at Brahmagiri in the District of Chitaldrug (over 300 still survive) that largely though not exclusively determined the Survey's extensive exploration of the area in 1947. But 1000 megalithic cists might be scrupulously excavated without any significant addition to our knowledge of their chronology. Only by placing their culture in a related culture-sequence, such as an adjacent town-site could alone be expected to provide, was it possible to ensure a substantive advance of knowledge. Brahmagiri with its vast field of megaliths amidst the named and dated ruins of the town of Isila appeared therefore to supply the essential coincidence required for an initial scientific study of the Indian megalithic problem. And so it proved.

In the region of Brahmagiri, some 600 feet above the plain, are no fewer than three adjacent copies of Aśoka's Minor Rock-edict no. 1 cut in 257 BC, manifestly marking the most southerly point of this great king's empire. The northern slopes of the hill also bear extensive signs of ancient occupation in the form of potsherds (including Arikamedu types), fragmentary walls, and remains of terraced platforms roughly levelled with dry-stone walling. In the midst of the zone of occupation stands a great boulder bearing on its upper surface the best-preserved of the three copies of the Edict, the so-called Brahmagiri version, carrying Aśoka's statement that the memorial was 'issued so that even my borderers may know that the instructions

37 General view north-west over the excavations of the ancient town, Isila, at Brahmagiri, 1947–8.

are directed to the Mahāmātras at Isila', incidentally denoting that the name of the ancient border-township thereabouts was Isila.

A series of pits dug archaeologically in the form of single or conjoined twenty-foot squares on the Isila town-site on our 'Taxila' method revealed a clearly stratified sequence of three cultures ranged from bottom to top as follows, but interlocked by significant overlaps. In other words the three cultures represent a continuous occupation of the site through three successive phases and can therefore be interrelated chronologically.

I *The Brahmagiri Stone Axe Culture* is a crude Chalcolithic culture with hand-made pottery extending down to a maximum height of nine feet from the natural surface, and conjecturally dated from the early first millennium B C (?) to the beginning of the second century B C or the approximate beginning of the Megalithic Culture. The industrial complex is characterized by polished pointed-butt axes of trap rock, associated with numerous crude microliths of jasper, flint, agate, etc., with a little copper or bronze, but no iron. The pottery is invariably hand-made, and there are a number of child-burials in urns.

II *The Megalithic Culture*, intrusive, first introduced iron-working to the locality, and was well supplied with tools and weapons (iron sickles, knives, swords, spears, and arrowheads, polished stone axes and microliths, probably survivals or overlaps). Distinctive pottery, polished but turned on the slow wheel, was characteristically black inside and black or red outside. No stone walls. Conjectural date-bracket, after *c.* 200 B C to the middle of the first century A D, overlapping the Āndhra Culture.

III *The Āndhra or Sātavāhana Culture*, sophisticated pottery with iron industries similar to those of the local megalithic tombs. The Āndhra deposits at Brahmagiri or Isila were at the same time in 1947 verified and amplified some miles away by a subsidiary excavation at a contemporary site known traditionally as Chandravalli or Moon-village in a once thickly occupied townlet now on the fringe of the district-town of Chitaldrug, where an abundant potin and silver (Roman) coinage and a spread of Āndhra and Arikamedu pottery promised cross-checks in our developing time-table. Nor were we disappointed. A rich yield of potin coinage was supported by upwards of five Roman denarii of the first half of the first century A D, thus conveniently filling material gaps in two links of our previous diagnostic evidence and in the process providing a welcome over-all sample of the skilfully manufactured and ornamented Āndhra wares which have now become invaluable interregional criteria over large areas of the Deccan between the first centuries B C and A D. A

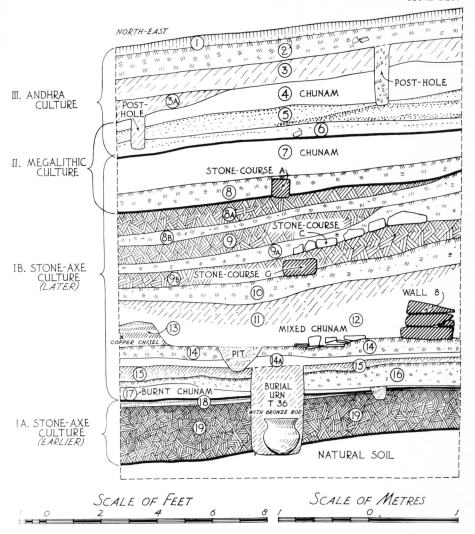

SOUTH-WEST

NORTH-EAST

POST-HOLE

III. ANDHRA CULTURE

POST-HOLE

④ CHUNAM

③A

⑤

⑥

II. MEGALITHIC CULTURE

⑦ CHUNAM

STONE-COURSE A

⑧

⑧A

STONE-COURSE C

⑧B

⑨

⑨A

IB. STONE-AXE CULTURE (LATER)

⑨B STONE-COURSE G

⑩

WALL 8

⑪

⑫

MIXED CHUNAM

⑬

COPPER CHISEL

⑭

PIT

⑭A

⑭

⑮

⑮

⑯

⑰ BURNT CHUNAM

⑱

BURIAL URN T 36 WITH BRONZE ROD

IA. STONE-AXE CULTURE (EARLIER)

⑲

⑲

NATURAL SOIL

SCALE OF FEET

0   2   4   6   8

SCALE OF METRES

0   1

38 Section through the site at Brahmagiri, 1947, showing the interrelationship of the different cultures.

65

recurrent feature of the ware is the use of salt-glaze with rectilinear criss-cross decoration in white (lime) under a wash of russet-coloured ochre. Note that whilst interchange of pottery types occurs at Brahmagiri and Chandravalli, coinage is restricted to the latter, where it is presumably an index of greater or at least more accessible local wealth.

In India it is possible to dig almost anywhere below a living level and to discover the vestiges of civilization, layer upon layer. That is not of course true of a great many regions of the world. Large expanses of Africa, for example, would be singularly unresponsive to a crude test of that sort! Which, needless to say, is not to affirm any contentious depreciation of the astonishing additions to human knowledge with which Africa, particularly north, east and south, has been constantly rewarding in other fields of science. But in India it may serve at least as a terminal explanation, or even apology, for consigning the famous riverine 'Indus Civilization' to the narrow limits of a postscript alongside the great Alexander who was uniquely armed amongst philosophers and won through when the heroic Herakles and the divine Dionysos had alike failed convincingly to lead the way.

CHAPTER SEVEN

The Indus Civilization

The plains of northern India are firmly framed towards the west by the almost vertebrate outline of the mighty Indus; otherwise, towards the east they are somewhat less sturdily subdivided by a liberal complex of ribs or tributaries which, with varying constancy, have long regulated distribution and administration, with aid from former supplementary rivers (the Sarasvati and Wahindat) which have been described as 'rivals' to the Indus between the sub-montane regions of the north-east and the Arabian Sea.

It is to one of the major Indus tributaries, the Ravi, that we may turn first, passing from Lahore to Montgomery, where after a further fifteen miles we pause and turn north-eastwards to the little country-town of HARAPPĀ which overlies and adjoins the sandy mounds of a derelict settlement, anciently several miles in circuit. It is possible that the old name of the place was Hari-Yūpūyā, which is twice mentioned in the Rigveda as the scene of an Aryan victory over a non-Aryan tribe. The site was first reported in 1826 by Charles Masson and was later recognized more adequately by General Alexander Cunningham as that of a considerable Chalcolithic city. Subsequently it was somewhat summarily excavated between 1920 and 1934. But meanwhile, in and after the middle of the century, it had been discovered that the Harappā mounds were full of ancient bricks, just such as were then urgently required as ballast for the construction of the Multan-Lahore railway, for which they were promptly used in quantity, to the sorry detriment of the ruins which the mounds contained. It was not indeed until after 1944 that modern archaeological methods were applied; and since by this time Harappā had become recognized as one of the major 'type-sites' of the Indus Civilization, it now attracted afresh the attention of the Archaeological Survey in circumstances which fall within the compass of the present book and so may be briefly recounted.

It was, I recall, on a warm May night in 1944 that a four miles' tonga-ride brought me as the newly appointed Director General of the Archaeological Survey with my local Muslim officer from a little railway-station labelled 'Harappā' along a deep sand track to a small rest-house beside the moonlit mounds of the ancient site. Warned by my anxious colleague that we must start our inspection at 5.30 next morning and finish by 7.30 'after which it would be too hot', we turned in with the dark figure of the *punka-walla* crouched patiently in the entrance and the night air rent by innumerable jackals in the neighbouring wilderness.

Next morning, punctually at 5.30, our little procession started out towards the sandy heaps. Within ten minutes I stopped and rubbed my eyes as I gazed upon the tallest mound, scarcely trusting my vision. Six hours later my embarrassed staff and I were still toiling with picks and knives under the blazing sun, the mad sahib (I am afraid) setting a relentless pace. To explain what had happened, I must deviate for a moment into Indus Valley archaeology. To do so will be not merely to prepare the way for our next steps at Harappā but to define initially certain important general principles of the planning and policies embodied in the Indus Civilization as a whole.

First, in anticipation let it be stated that within the great expanse of the Civilization, covering in all an appreciably larger area than any of the equivalent early civilizations, there were two cities of outstanding size and presumably in some manner metropolitan: first HARAPPĀ in the Punjab where a moment or two ago we were strangely labouring in the midday sun, and secondly MOHENJO-DARO beside the main stream of the Indus in Sind, to which we shall turn anon. Both of the great cities were something like three miles in circumference; both were thought to be devoid of fortifications. Accordingly, prior to 1944 there was a tendency to regard the Indus

39 The 'melted' mud-brick towers of Harappā before excavation, 1946.

Civilization as something extraneous to the normal trend of the aristocratic or bureaucratic king- and priest-ridden societies further west, in Mesopotamia, Anatolia and Egypt. This apparently heterogeneous character, strangely anachronistic in the Chalcolithic age, was stressed by Gordon Childe in his *New Light on the Most Ancient East* (London, 1934):

No multiplication of weapons of war and battle-scenes attests futile conflicts between city-states as in Babylonia nor yet the force whereby a single king, as in Egypt, achieved by conquest internal peace and warded off jealous nomads by constant preparedness. We cannot even define the nucleus round which accumulated the surplus wealth of capital involved in the conversion of the village into the city. . . . No temple nor palace dominates the rest

though the total areas excavated would compare favourably with those explored in Mesopotamia. The visitor inevitably gets an impression of a democratic bourgeois economy. . . .

This Elysian polity, not altogether perhaps devoid of a Marxist flavour, seemed too good to be true but was not on that account false. There was little in the printed evidence to contradict it. But the printed evidence was in fact singularly incomplete.

As I approached the highest mound on that May morning the truth, or a part of the truth, of the matter stood suddenly revealed to me in the strong sloping light of the early sun. The mound was fringed with great piled masses of yellow mud which could scarcely be other than monsoon-riven brickwork. Nay more; a little scraping showed up the actual joints, and doubt was out of the question. The mound, standing high above the adjacent heaps, had been barricaded by a great brick wall. The city, so far from being an unarmed sanctuary of peace, was dominated by the towers and battlements of a lofty man-made acropolis of defiantly feudal aspect. Two years later, when we returned to conduct a major excavation, the details of a commanding work of military engineering were uncovered in convincing detail.

It is not my purpose here to collect in any detail the accumulative evidence which scraps of excavation by others of varying re-sponsibility had begun to assemble at Harappā prior to our work there in and after 1944. It will perhaps suffice if for general purposes then and after that date I may refer in the present context to my *Indus Civilization* (Cambridge, 1968), leaving to others the disappointing vestiges bequeathed by the systematic brick-robbery to which I have referred. Nevertheless, it was at Harappā that, in spite of the absence of a recovered street-plan, the essential make-up of the Indus Valley cities was first recognized after 1946. Harappā it was that first produced a hint of an organic antecedent culture, with more than a hint of a successor, and in that year it was the only known Harappan site which was thus bracketed. There too for the first time, in spite of widespread destruction, the main features of a typical Harappan

40 Section through the mud-brick rampart of
Harappā, built on a base 40 ft wide. The lower
figure stands on the original natural surface.

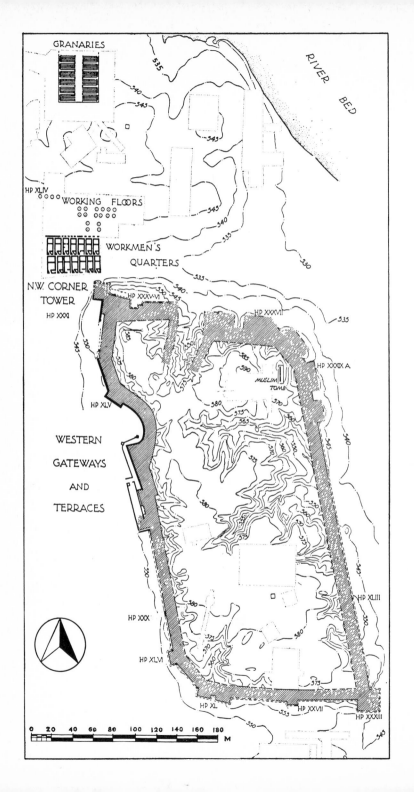

GRANARIES

RIVER BED

HP XLIV

WORKING FLOORS

WORKMEN'S
QUARTERS

N.W. CORNER
TOWER

HP XXXI

HP XXXV-VI

HP XXXVII

HP XXXIX A

MUSLIM
TOMB

HP XLV

WESTERN

GATEWAYS

AND

TERRACES

HP XLIII

HP XXX

HP XLVI

HP XL

HP XXVII

HP XXXIII

0 20 40 60 80 100 120 140 160 180
M

town-plan were at last becoming intelligible: on the west stood the high bulk of the towered citadel; towards the east and south lay the cemeteries and the ragged mounds of the 'lower city'; to the north could be seen a slightly hollowed belt containing notably verdant crops marking an old bed of the Ravi (now flowing six miles further north) which anciently supplied the old city with fish and transport from its wandering course; and between the citadel and the river-bed was an orderly cantonment, including a double range of granaries, another double range of barrack-like dwellings and some eighteen circular brick platforms designed to carry grinding-mills. For the rest the ground is littered with broken walls and floors, which have been neither intelligently excavated nor planned.

41 (*left*) Plan of the citadel of Harappā, fortified with mud-brick ramparts revetted with baked brick and, to the north, the granaries.

42 A brick platform at Harappā, with socket for former wooden grinding-mill.

43, 44 (*overleaf*) Typical potsherds from Harappā.

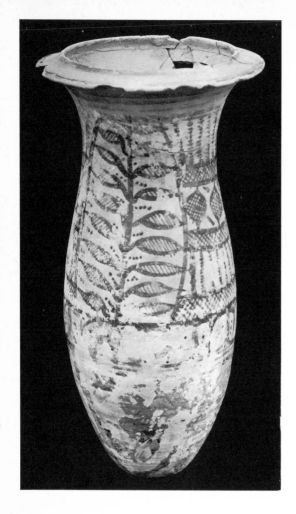

45 Black-painted red
vase from Harappā.

From Harappā we turn now sharply south-westwards from the
Punjab to Sind where some 400 miles away, in the district of Larkānā,
we would reach the environs of the river Indus and the crumbling
brick ruins of Mohenjo-daro, the second of our great Indus cities. As
we travelled my official companion put me into the local picture,
which was roughly as follows. My Muslim officer began a trifle
unexpectedly and anxiously with the words: 'Sahib, tonight big
moon. Must have care'. Prodded with questions he reluctantly went

on to explain that we should in due course leave the train at a wayside station and travel then in a tonga by a country-road eight miles to the ancient site where there was a rest-house for the night. To further questions he replied again: 'We must take care, sahib. Dacoits'. It eventually appeared that a gang of about fifteen of these pests was working the Mohenjo-daro region and we must have special care. It then occurred to me that four or five years previously one of my predecessors had been shot and killed by dacoits intent on robbery as he emerged from his tent in the Baluch foothills at dawn. 'What did my companion suggest that we should do about this tiresome situation?' Trees and paddy-fields surrounded the nearby rest-house and enlarged the complication. 'But', he added hopefully, 'we can sleep on the roof?' An hour later I found that in fact a somewhat precarious flight of external steps provided some sort of approach to altitude and security. The scene round about, enclosed by closely-packed tamarisk and babul trees, was brilliantly moon-lit and completely theatrical as we all of us lay down closely on the flat roof. As I said good-night to my little party I thought it sensible to omit any reference to the revolver which bulged one of my pockets, and we slept peacefully enough through a somewhat noisy but otherwise uninterrupted night. A few days later a cautious Indian Government provided me with a permanent guard of four Gurkhas who under my watchful eye thereafter accompanied my headquarters throughout India. They were amiable fellows and useful as additional baggage-carriers. But they never had cause to go into action!

On the occasion of my first night at Mohenjo-daro on the rest-house roof, I recall how the slowly growing light of the pre-dawn dimly showed through the verdure at a distance of some two furlongs from our point of vantage a tall mound crowned, as we discovered, by the considerable wreckage of a Buddhist shrine or stupa, perhaps of the second century AD, raised high upon the heaped remains of an earlier age. As we climbed towards the basic mound, now lighted by the rising sun, elements of the scene before and beneath us began to assume a strongly reminiscent meaning. Here in this high mound,

apart from its extraneous capping, was surely a repetition of the flanking citadel which a day or two earlier we had been recognizing for the first time at Harappā, together with a hint of its revolutionary implication. But it was not at once that Mohenjo-daro began to reveal its full story. For that we had to wait a further half-dozen years and changing environmental circumstance – actually until 1950, when the new state of Pakistan had assumed the proprietorship of Sind and the administrative responsibilities which accompanied it. These included the specialized duties involved in the maintenance and

46 General view of the
Mohenjo-daro citadel, still
crowned by the 2nd-century-
AD Buddhist shrine or stupa
which overlies the earlier
Harappan site.

further exploration of the State's antiquities amongst which those
represented by Mohenjo-daro ranked first in order amongst the
prehistoric vestiges of the region, and the most urgent in matters
relating to conversation and record. Many years of industrious work
under the old régime, however well-intentioned, had left more
problems than it had scientifically solved. Amongst them were those
of the re-shaping of the Indus cities along the lines of which a
preliminary hint, but no more than a hint, had been given, as we have
seen, by our preliminary work at Harappā.

CHAPTER EIGHT

Pakistan, 1947–1950

First amongst our new problems in 1947 was that of creating from zero an adequately efficient Pakistani Archaeological Department from such scraps as could be brought together on the spur of the moment. I may be forgiven if I say that the first of these scraps was myself who, having completed my tour of duty in the old India, was now invited by the new Pakistan to serve awhile as adviser – blessed word – in the creation and training of a new all-purposes archaeological staff.

As an initial nucleus from Bengal and the Punjab I gathered together a dozen or more young officers and assistants of my old Department of Archaeology with a leavening of useful university students to whom an unexpected but in the circumstance peculiarly welcome bonus was added in the person of a young Oxford graduate who arrived voluntarily upon the scene happily equipped with experience in the Indian army and a modicum of archaeological training in England combined with a wholehearted interest in the multiple problems which lay before us. The name of Leslie Alcock has more recently become familiar in certain Welsh and Scottish universities, but at the time of which I am speaking he quickly found himself closely involved in our Pakistan affairs and was an invaluable aid in our training operations as an articulate lecturer and an active instructor in archaeological methodology. In particular he no doubt recalls as vividly as the rest of us the major excavation upon which he proceeded to concentrate our first efforts at Mohenjo-daro where, as has been recalled above, we had recognized shortly after my first arrival what could only be the equivalent of our Harappā citadel.

47 Bronze dancing-girl from Mohenjo-daro; the figurine is naked except for her necklace and bangles.

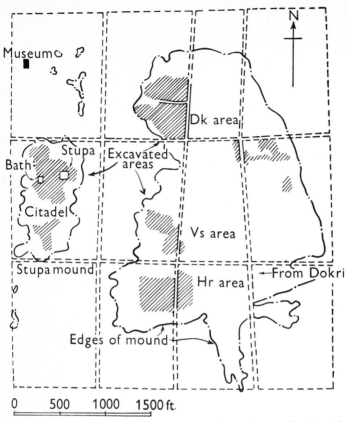

Museum☉ ♂
■ ·3

Stupa
Bath·
Citadel
Dk area
Excavated areas
Vs area
Hr area
From Dokri
Stupa mound
Edges of mound

N

0   500   1000   1500 ft.

48, 49 Suggested original layout of Mohenjo-daro, with a detail (*right*) showing the citadel.

Subsequently a detailed examination of the steep flanks of the newly discovered Mohenjo-daro mound revealed uncertain vestiges of baked brickwork which demanded investigation with all skills that could be rallied. Accordingly our inexperienced new staff in March and April 1950 aided by a gang of local peasants was focused upon the scene for combined discovery and training. With the gradual removal of sand and debris the few bricks originally detected grew into many until the stark walls of a huge platform began to emerge from the hillside. The aspect was that of a fortress, towering grim and forbidding above the plain. And yet . . . I wondered.

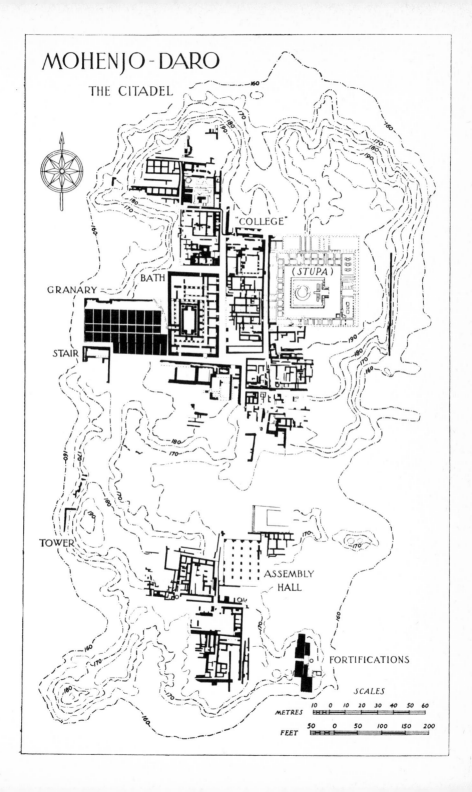

MOHENJO-DARO

THE CITADEL

"COLLEGE"

(STUPA)

GRANARY

BATH

STAIR

TOWER

ASSEMBLY
HALL

FORTIFICATIONS

SCALES

METRES

FEET

50 The excavation workforce at Mohenjo-daro, 1950.
Key to names: 1 Leslie Alcock; 2 Wali Ullah Khan,
foreman; 3 Sadar Din, foreman; 4 R.E.M.W.;
5 Manlvi Shamshud Ali, Acting Director of
Archaeology, Pakistan; 6 Ahmed Hassan Dahni,
Superintendent in the Dept. of Archaeology;
7 Fazal Ahmed Khan, subsequently Director
of Archaeology, Pakistan.

51 Part of the brick platform on which the original timber granary of Mohenjo-daro once stood. The lower figures show how the grain, brought in as tribute from the adjacent countryside, was hauled up on to the main loading-platform; the other figure (top left) is crouching in the opening of one of the ventilation ducts.

The work proceeded with the meticulous controls proper to a teaching-operation but with astonishing productiveness. Stratified potsherds and other objects were recovered and recorded literally by the ton; four weeks after the beginning, twelve wagon-loads of selected pottery were sent back to base, and more followed. And day by day the sullen brick structure frowned upon us in growing complexity and immensity. A grid of strange passages had appeared in it, signs of a one-time superstructure of timber, and a curious platform alongside with a carefully designed approach. In spite of its starkness, the structure became less and less like a fortress, but what

52–6 The artisans of Mohenjo-daro were masters of a variety of different media. Precious stone necklaces (*above left*) show links with ancient Western civilizations, but other artifacts are of indigenous origin: a terracotta figurine of a 'mother-goddess' (*above right*) bedecked with jewellery; a seal impression of an ox-like creature (*left*) standing before a manger or incense-burner; and a terracotta ox (*below left*) and buffalo (*below right*).

was it? Nothing short of complete excavation was now likely to unfold the secret. We took another village upon our strength and fairly hurled ourselves into the task amidst the hot brickwork, drawing, planning, recording as we went with something almost approaching desperation. Then suddenly the problem answered itself.

I was returning from a hurried visit to my Minister at Karachi. It was 2 a.m. once more in bright moonlight when I reached the little wayside station eight miles from Mohenjo-daro, to be met by my locum tenens Alcock in our jeep. 'Well', I said, almost unthinkingly, 'how is the civic granary?' He looked a trifle startled, but by the end of the eight miles we had argued it backwards and forwards, and were of one mind. The high podium on the accessible flank of the citadel (away from the town), the grid of air-ducts to dry the floor of the great timber barn which had at one time crowned it, the loading-platform, the carefully planned approach for the wagons bringing in the tributary corn – every detail fell into place. Set prominently amidst the royal or municipal buildings of the acropolis, this had been the economic focus of the city, equivalent to the State Treasury of later times, register of the city's wealth and well-being.´ A new chapter had been added to the story of the metropolis.

Our work was done and our training-establishment went steadily ahead as we toiled through the hot days and lectured to one another in the cooler evenings within the approximate shelter of a large tent dimly lit by a pressure-lamp and lively discussion. I think it may be claimed that on the whole our Mohenjo-daro School in 1950 proceeded and ended with a sense of not inadequate achievement comparable with that which half-a-dozen years earlier had favoured and distinguished our combined effort at Taxila in the Punjab and is still a treasured domestic memory in the annals of Subcontinental Archaeology. Incidentally it may serve as a finale to this collection of random memories, covering six or seven years of progressive archaeology within something like a million square miles of southern Asia.

88

Appendix

The scope and personnel of the Survey

Any record of the shaping and growth of the widespread activities of the Archaeological Survey of India between 1944 and 1976 would be sadly incomplete without the inclusion of a partial list of senior officers who have variously contributed to this achievement, culminating in the present (1976) Director General of Archaeology, Shri M. N. Deshpande, a former pupil of the Taxila School, who today holds the senior archaeological post together with that of Joint Secretary to the Government of India. Preceding him as Director General may be included Dr N. P. Chakravati (1948–50), Shri A. Ghosh (1953–68), Shri B. B. Lal (1968–72), with the addition in 1975 of Shri B. K. Thapar as Joint Director General, whilst other seniors are nowadays commonly graded as Superintending Archaeologists with territorial assignations in eleven 'Circles' (such as Central Circle from Bhopal, Eastern Circle from Calcutta, Frontier Circle from Srinagar, Mid-Eastern Circle from Patna, Northern Circle from Agra, North-Eastern Circle from Dehra Dun, Southern Circle from Madras, South-Western Circle from Aurangabad, etc.).

Mention should also be made of the Survey's School of Archaeology, now under the direction of Shri K.V. Soundara Rajan. The School is still much sought after for training students not only from India but likewise from neighbouring countries such as Nepal, Burma, Indonesia, Ceylon and Afghanistan as well. Other specialists over a wide range include the Government Epigraphist, with particularized branches in Sanskrit or Dravidian or Arabic, Persian, etc. Another significant development in recent years has been the work taken up by the Survey outside India, such as that done by

Departmental conservators at Bamiyan and Balkh where it has brought credit to the Survey and has encouraged the opening up of field-research by Indian archaeologists in Afghanistan for which preparation is now under way. Specific studies or duties fall under the Director for Monuments (Dr (Smt) D. Mitra); the Director of Antiquities (Dr N. R. Banerjee); the Director of Explorations (Shri J. P. Joshi); the Director of Expeditions Abroad (Shri H. Sarkar); the Chief Archaeological Engineer (Shri R. Sengupta); the Superintending Archaeologist (Special) (Shri T. N. Khazanchi); the Excavations Branch (under Shri K. M. Srivastava and Shri M. G. Joshi); the Chief Archaeological Chemist (Shri J. C. Nagpal); the Prehistory Branch (under Dr K. D. Banerjee); the Museums Branch at Calcutta (under Shri K. R. Vijayaraghavan); the Gardens Branch (under Shri S. N. Singh) at Agra; with Shri Abong Imlong as General Director of Administration at headquarters.

Select bibliography

ALLCHIN, BRIDGET AND RAYMOND, *The Birth of Indian Civilization,* Harmondsworth, 1968

SMITH, VINCENT A., *The Oxford History of India,* 3rd edn., Oxford, 1958.

WHEELER, R. E. M., *Five Thousand Years of Pakistan in Archaeological Outline,* London, 1950
— *Rome Beyond the Imperial Frontiers,* London, 1954, New York, 1955
— *Chārsada, a Metropolis of the North-West Frontier,* Oxford, 1962
— *Civilizations of the Indus Valley and Beyond,* London and New York, 1966
— *The Indus Civilization,* 3rd edn., Cambridge, 1968
— *Early India and Pakistan,* revised edn., London and New York, 1969
— 'Roman Contact with India, Pakistan and Afghanistan', in Grimes, W. F. (ed.), *Aspects of Archaeology, Essays presented to O.G.S. Crawford,* London, 1951, pp. 345–81

List of illustrations

Index

23 Group of students at the Taxila School measuring pottery, 1944. *Photo Archaeological Survey of India.*

24 Four silver denarii of Augustus from a hoard found at Eyyal near Trichur, Cochin State, South India.

25 Map showing the distribution of Roman coins in India.

26 Arretine and imitation Arretine ware of 1st century AD, found at Arikamedu, South India. Ht. of sherd bottom right 4·5 cms. ($1\frac{3}{4}$ ins.).

27 View north-east across the lagoon towards Arikamedu, 1945.

28 Indo-Roman brick foundations projecting from the river-bank at Arikamedu, 1945. *Photo Archaeological Survey of India.*

29 Excavations at Arikamedu, 1945. *Photo Archaeological Survey of India.*

30 VIBII potter's stamp on sherd of Arretine ware, 1st century AD. Found at Arikamedu, 1945. *Photo Archaeological Survey of India.*

31 Roman amphorae fragments from Arikamedu, 1945. Max. ht. 32·5 cms. (13 ins.).

32 Rouletted ware, 1st century AD, from Brahmagiri, Chitaldrug district, Mysore. Diam. of bowl 17 cms. ($6\frac{3}{4}$ ins.).

33 Map showing ports and markets in India in the 1st century AD.

34 Map showing distribution of megalithic cists in India.

35 Megalithic cist with 'port-hole', Vengupattu, North Arcot district. *Photo Archaeological Survey of India.*

36 A 'port-hole' megalithic cist excavated at Brahmagiri, 1947–8.

37 General view north-west over the excavations at Brahmagiri, 1947–8.

38 Section through Brahmagiri, 1947, showing interrelationship of cultures.

39 The north-east corner of the site at Harappā, before excavation, 1946.

40 A section of the mud-brick rampart, Harappā, 1946–7.

41 Plan of citadel of Harappā.

42 Brick grinding-mill platform at Harappā, 1946–7.

43, 44 Potsherds of 3rd–2nd millennium BC, from Harappā. Max. ht. 14 cms. ($5\frac{1}{2}$ ins.).

45 Vase of 3rd–2nd millennium BC, from Harappā. Ht. 29 cms. ($11\frac{1}{2}$ ins.).

46 General view of the Mohenjo-daro citadel.

47 Bronze dancing-girl from Mohenjo-daro. Ht. 10 cms. (4 ins.). National Museum of India, New Delhi.

48 Plan of the suggested original layout of Mohenjo-daro. After Stuart Piggott.

49 Plan of the citadel at Mohenjo-daro.

50, 50a The workforce at Mohenjo-daro, 1950, with key.

51 Brick base of granary at Mohenjo-daro, showing loading bay.

52 Precious stone necklace from Mohenjo-daro.

53 Terracotta 'mother goddess' figurine from Mohenjo-daro. National Museum of Pakistan.

54 Seal impression with ox-like creature from Mohenjo-daro. Ht. 6·5 cms. ($2\frac{1}{2}$ ins.).

55,56 Terracotta ox and buffalo from Mohenjo-daro. Hts. 7 cms. ($2\frac{3}{4}$ ins.).

Index